Sa

Novena and Prayers

By
Mary Mark Wickenhiser, FSP

Pauline
BOOKS & MEDIA
Boston

Nihil Obstat: Rev. Thomas W. Buckley

Imprimatur: ✠ Most Rev. Seán O'Malley, O.F.M.Cap.
Archbishop of Boston
January 19, 2004

ISBN 0-8198-7080-3

Cover design by Rosana Usselmann

Cover art by Tracy L. Christianson

Texts of the New Testament used in this work are taken from The *St. Paul Catholic Edition of the New Testament*, translated by Mark A. Wauck. Copyright © 1992, Society of St. Paul. All rights reserved.

Texts of the Psalms used in this work are translated by Manuel Miguens. Copyright © 1995, Daughters of St. Paul.

Published by Pauline Books & Media, 50 Saint Pauls Avenue, Boston MA 02130-3491. www.pauline.org

Printed in the U.S.A.

Pauline Books & Media is the publishing house of the Daughters of St. Paul, an international congregation of women religious serving the Church with the communications media.

6 7 8 9 10 11   20 19 18 17 16

Contents

What Is a Novena?

The Catholic tradition of praying novenas has its roots in the earliest days of the Church. In the Acts of the Apostles we read that after the ascension of Jesus, the apostles returned to Jerusalem, to the upper room, where "They all devoted themselves single-mindedly to prayer, along with some women and Mary the Mother of Jesus and his brothers" (Acts 1:14). Jesus had instructed his disciples to wait for the coming of the Holy Spirit, and on the day of Pentecost, the Spirit of the Lord came to them. This prayer of the first Christian community was the first "novena." Based on this, Christians have always prayed for various needs, trusting that God both hears and answers prayer.

The word "novena" is derived from the Latin term *novem*, meaning nine. In biblical times numbers held deep symbolism for people. The number "three," for example, symbolized perfection, fullness, completeness. The number nine—three times three—symbolized perfection times perfection. Novenas developed because it was thought that—symbolically speaking—nine days represented the perfect amount of time to pray. The ancient Greeks and Romans had the custom of mourning for nine days after a death. The early Christian Church offered Mass for the deceased for nine consecutive days. During the Middle Ages novenas in preparation for solemn feasts became popular, as did novenas to particular saints.

Whether a novena is made solemnly—in a parish church in preparation for a feastday—or in the privacy of one's home, as Christians we never really pray alone. Through the waters of Baptism we have become members of the Body of Christ and are thereby united to every other member of Christ's Mystical Body. When we pray, we are spiritually united with all the other members.

Just as we pray for each other while here on earth, those who have gone before us and are united with God in heaven can pray for us and intercede for us as well. We Catholics use the term "communion of saints" to refer to this exchange of spiritual help among the members of the Church on earth, those who have died and are being purified, and the saints in heaven.

While nothing can replace the celebration of Mass and the sacraments as the Church's highest form of prayer, devotions have a special place in

Catholic life. Devotions such as the Stations of the Cross can help us enter into the sufferings of Jesus and give us an understanding of his personal love for us. The mysteries of the rosary can draw us into meditating on the lives of Jesus and Mary. Devotions to the saints can help us witness to our faith and encourage us in our commitment to lead lives of holiness and service as they did.

How to use this booklet

*T*he morning and evening prayers are modeled on the Liturgy of the Hours, following its pattern of psalms, scripture readings, and intercessions.

We suggest that during the novena you make time in your schedule to pray the morning prayer and evening prayer. If you are able, try to also set aside a time during the day when you can pray the novena and any other particular prayer(s) you have chosen. Or you can recite the devotional prayers at the conclusion of the morning or evening prayer. What is important is to pray with expectant faith and confidence in a loving God who will answer our prayers in the way that will most benefit us. The Lord "satisfies the thirsty, and the hungry he fills with good things" (Ps 107:9).

St. Joseph

The Gospels do not tell us much about Joseph—just enough to help us realize his special place in God's plan of salvation. Although none of his words are recorded, we learn that Joseph "*did* as the angel of the Lord had commanded him" (Mt 1:24). His faith and willing cooperation with God's plan make him a model for all Christians.

In his apostolic exhortation, *Guardian of the Redeemer*, Pope John Paul II has given a comprehensive teaching on the person and mission of St. Joseph in the life of the Church. The pope calls him the "guardian of the mystery of God," referring to Joseph's special role as the foster father of Jesus. Quoting St. Augustine, the pope notes that, "By reason of their faithful marriage *both of them* deserve to be called Christ's parents, not only his mother, but also his father, who was a parent in the same way that he was the mother's spouse: *in mind,* not in the flesh." Although not his biological father, Joseph exercised a true fatherhood with regard to Jesus in every other way. He cared for him, taught him a trade, and formed him in the religious traditions of Israel. Through Joseph, Jesus experienced the love of a human father.

Joseph was also the husband of Mary. The news about Mary's pregnancy evidently confused and disturbed him to the point that he decided not to go ahead with their plans for marriage. But an angelic messenger reassured him: "Joseph son of David, do not be afraid to take your wife Mary into your house—the child who has been conceived in her is from the Holy Spirit" (Mt 1:20). Joseph's marriage to Mary was an important part of God's plan. It was unique in that they remained virginal out of respect for the mystery that God had worked in Mary. Church teaching on Mary's perpetual virginity, however, is not intended to imply a negative attitude toward conjugal love, which is a great good. As Pope John Paul II explains: "There are really two kinds of love here, both of which together represent the mystery of the Church—virgin and spouse—as symbolized in the marriage of Mary and Joseph. 'Virginity or celibacy for the sake of the kingdom of God not only does not contradict the dignity of marriage but presupposes and confirms it. Marriage and virginity are two ways of expressing and living the one mystery of the Covenant of God with his people,' the Covenant which is a communion of love between God and human beings" (*Guardian of the Redeemer*, n. 20, quoting *Role of the Christian Family*, n. 16).

As husband and father, Joseph faithfully lived out God's plan for his life. He gave Mary and Jesus the gift of his love, sacrificing himself through hard work and dedication. The Gospel tells us that he was a carpenter. He taught Jesus his trade, showing us the value of work done out of love. For this reason, the Church venerates Joseph as the patron of workers, celebrating a feast of Joseph the Worker on May 1.

Joseph also shows us the importance of prayer and the value of a deep spiritual life. Living with Mary, who "kept all these things in her heart" (Lk 2:51), and with Jesus, God Incarnate, Joseph certainly had the opportunity to reflect on these mysteries in prayer. As devout Jews, the Holy Family attended the religious services of their people and heard the Scriptures proclaimed. The Gospel notes that Jesus attended the synagogue, "as was his custom" (Lk 4:16), a custom he learned, no doubt, from Joseph. When St. Teresa of Avila set out to renew the Carmelite Order, she put her work under the protection of St. Joseph, seeing in him a model of prayer and contemplation.

In 1870, Pope Pius IX proclaimed Joseph patron of the universal Church. Just as he protected and watched over the Holy Family, he watches over the Church from heaven. The Church asks for his help and follows his example as it carries out its mission in the world. Joseph is also venerated as a model for laborers, the saint of divine providence, and the patron of a holy death. His feastday is March 19.

Marianne Lorraine Trouvé, FSP

Morning Prayer

*M*orning prayer is a time to give praise and thanks to God, to remind ourselves that he is the source of all beauty and goodness. Lifting one's heart and mind to God in the early hours of the day puts one's life into perspective: God is our loving Creator who watches over us with tenderness and is always ready to embrace us with his compassion and mercy.

While at prayer, try to create a prayerful atmosphere, perhaps with a burning candle to remind you that Christ is the light who illumines your daily path, an open Bible to remind you that the Lord is always present, a crucifix to remind you of the depths of God's love for you. Soft music can also contribute to a serene and prayerful mood.

If a quiet place is not available, or if you pray as you commute to and from work, remember that the God who loves you is present everywhere and hears your prayer no matter the setting.

I will bless the Lord at all times,
his praise will be ever on my lips.
Glory be to the Father, and to the Son, and to the
Holy Spirit,
as it was in the beginning, is now, and will be
forever. Amen

Psalm 92

It is good to praise and thank the Lord.

It is good to give thanks to the LORD,
to sing psalms to your name, Most High;
to declare your loving kindness in the morning
and your faithfulness every night,
with the sound of a ten-stringed lyre,
and the music of a harp.
For you, LORD, have made me rejoice because of
your works,
I shout for joy at the works of your hands.
How great, O LORD, are your deeds,
how deep your designs.

Glory be to the Father…

Psalm 112

The Lord blesses those who love him.
Happy are those who fear the LORD,
who joyfully keep of his commandments.
Their children will be powerful in the land;
the descendants of the upright shall be blessed.
Their righteous conduct shall stand forever.
Merciful, compassionate, and righteous,
in the darkness they rise like a light for the up-
    right.
The righteous will be held in everlasting remem-
    brance.
They will never be afraid of bad reports,
their hearts are steadfast for they trust in the LORD.
Lavishly they sow and give to the poor;
their righteousness endures forever.

Glory be to the Father…

The Word of God
Matthew 6:19–21

Living in God's presence gives genuine purpose to our lives. When we keep our priorities straight and put

God in first place, earthly goods will not become the central focus of our lives. Instead, the things of this earth become stepping-stones to God.

*D*o not store up treasures for yourselves on earth,
where moth and rust destroy,
and where thieves break in and steal;
Store up treasures for yourselves in Heaven,
where neither moth nor rust destroy,
and where thieves neither break in nor steal.
For where your treasure is,
there will your heart be too."

Open my heart, Lord, to the power of your word.

From prayer one draws the strength needed to meet the challenges of daily life as a committed follower of Jesus Christ and, as such, to be a living sign of the Lord's loving presence in the world.

Intercessions

*L*ord, I thank you for the gift of a new day, and I come into your presence to seek your grace and blessing:

Response: Lord, keep me mindful of your love today.

Open the eyes of my heart that I may recognize your loving Providence at work in the events of this day. **R.**

Inspire my thoughts, words, and actions that I may be a source of joy and consolation for all those I meet today. **R.**

Be with me today so that in all I say and do, I may be a living witness of your love and mercy. **R.**

Grant that all those I love may be kept from harm this day. **R.**

(Add your own general intentions and your particular intentions for this novena.)

Conclude your intercessions by praying to our heavenly Father in the words Jesus taught us:

Our Father, who art in heaven, hallowed be thy name; thy kingdom come; thy will be done on earth as it is in heaven. Give us this day our daily bread, and forgive us our trespasses, as we forgive those who trespass against us, and lead us not into temptation, but deliver us from evil. Amen.

Closing Prayer

*F*ather in heaven, hear my morning prayer; let the splendor of your love light my way that I may spend this day in joy of spirit and peace of mind. Grant this through Christ, your Son. Amen.

Let us praise the Lord.
And give him thanks.

Devotion of the Seven Sundays

Devotion of the Seven Sundays to honor the seven sorrows and seven joys of St. Joseph may be practiced at any time of the year. Devotees of St. Joseph have followed the custom to venerate him especially on the seven Sundays preceding his feast.

The following practices are recommended for each Sunday: to participate in Mass and receive Holy Communion in honor of St. Joseph, to set aside time to contemplate the Scripture passages commemorating his seven sorrows and seven joys, and to offer these prayers in an attitude of praise and confidence.

In Honor of the Seven Sorrows and Joys of St. Joseph

First Sunday

Mary was betrothed to Joseph, but before they came together, she was found to be with child by the Holy Spirit. Joseph her husband was a good and upright man so he was planning to put her away, but quietly because he did not wish to disgrace her. But while he was thinking these things over, behold, an angel of the Lord appeared to him in a dream and said, "Joseph son of David, do not be afraid to take your wife Mary into your house—the child who has been conceived in her is from the Holy Spirit. She will give birth to a son and you shall name him Jesus, because he will save his people from their sins" (Mt 1:18–21).

St. Joseph, what anguish must have filled your heart when you thought of ending your betrothal to Mary, to "put her away" quietly and not disgrace her. And what profound joy you must have experienced when the mystery of the Incarnation was revealed to you. By this sorrow and joy of yours, I ask that you walk with me through the uncertainties in my life. Teach me how to surrender to the Lord the moments of confusion, to listen with my heart when the Spirit speaks to me so that, like you, I may accomplish all that the Lord has planned for me.

(Our Father, Hail Mary, Glory be…)

Second Sunday

Since Joseph was of the house and family of David he went up from Nazareth in Galilee to Bethlehem of Judea, the city of David, to be registered with Mary, who was betrothed to him and who was pregnant. It happened that while they were there the day came for her to give birth. She gave birth to her first-born son, wrapped him in swaddling clothes, and laid him in a manger, because there was no room for them in the inn (Lk 2:4–7).

St. Joseph, while chosen by God to be the foster father of the Word made flesh, you still suffered distress at having to accept the shelter of a stable for Mary to give birth. But the deprivation you experienced must have turned to joy when you heard angels heralding the birth of the Savior.

By this sorrow and joy of yours, I ask you to intercede before the Lord for those who are without food and shelter for themselves and their families. Ask our heavenly Father to open the hearts of the leaders of nations to understand and acknowledge the dignity of the human person, so that the necessities of life are provided for all God's children.

(Our Father, Hail Mary, Glory be…)

———————⌘———————

Third Sunday

And when eight days had passed for his circumcision they gave him the name Jesus, the name given him by the angel before he was conceived in the womb (Lk 2:21).

St. Joseph, even while you faithfully obeyed the Law, surely you were saddened at the sight of the blood shed by the Infant Savior at his circumcision. At the same time, the name "Jesus" must have filled you with new hope and profound joy.

By this sorrow and joy of yours, teach me to value the laws of God and the Church, and to always speak the name of Jesus with reverence.

Ask our heavenly Father to bless all children; may God grant them a vibrant faith to sustain them, an abiding hope to encourage them, and a steadfast love for Jesus to accompany them along life's way.

(Our Father, Hail Mary, Glory be…)

His father and mother were amazed at what was said about Jesus. And Simeon blessed them and said to his mother, Mary, "Behold, he is destined to bring about the fall and rise of many in Israel, and to be a sign that will be opposed (and a sword will pierce your own soul) so that the thoughts of many hearts may be revealed" (Lk 2:33–35).

St. Joseph, the words of Simeon must have gripped your heart with foreboding and perhaps even a sense of powerlessness to prevent the suffering that Mary must have endured when she heard the prophesy. Yet, what joy you must have felt knowing that the salvation foretold by Simeon would be offered to all peoples.

By this sorrow and joy of yours, ask the Lord to grant me a deeper trust in the promises God has made, so that I may proclaim the message of salvation through my words and actions.

(Our Father, Hail Mary, Glory be...)

Fifth Sunday

An angel of the Lord appeared in a dream to
Joseph and said, "Get up, take the child and
its mother and flee to Egypt and stay there
until I tell you—Herod is going to search for
the child to kill it." So Joseph got up and
took the child and its mother and departed
by night for Egypt, and he stayed there until
Herod's death... (Mt 2:13–15).

St. Joseph, attentive guardian of the incarnate
Son of God, you listened to the Spirit's inspiration
to flee to Egypt even though it meant hardship and
struggle. Still, because you were a caring parent and
devoted spouse, surely you rejoiced to have been
able to protect and provide for Jesus and Mary in an
unfamiliar and hostile land.

By this sorrow and joy of yours, obtain for me
the grace to always listen to the voice of my conscience urging me to follow after those things that
will lead to eternal happiness.

Intercede before the Lord for all those who are
forced to live in a strange land, those who are poor
and in need, and those who are without a home or

employment. In their time of hardship be their protector and provider.

(*Our Father, Hail Mary, Glory be...*)

Sixth Sunday

After Herod died, an angel of the Lord appeared in a dream to Joseph in Egypt and said, "Get up, take the child and its mother and go to the land of Israel.... So Joseph got up and took the child and its mother and went into the land of Israel (Mt 2:19–21).

They returned to Galilee to their own city, Nazareth. The child grew and became strong and was filled with wisdom, and the grace of God was on him (Lk 2:39–40).

St. Joseph, your consolation in having brought Jesus and Mary safely out of the land of Egypt must have been burdened at times by the fear that Herod's successor would also seek out the Child to kill him. But despite your fear, you set about to live an ordinary and happy life at Nazareth in the company of Jesus and Mary, placing your trust in the Lord.

By this sorrow and joy of yours, obtain for me the grace of an abiding confidence in God. In difficult circumstances teach me how to recognize the Lord's will for myself and my family, so that all that I do, however hidden or simple, may reflect your love.

(Our Father, Hail Mary, Glory be…)

Seventh Sunday

And it happened that after three days they found him in the Temple, seated in the midst of the teachers…. When his parents saw him they were amazed, and his mother said to him, "Son, why did you do this to us? You see your father and I have been looking for you, worried to death!" And he said to them, "Why were you looking for me? Did you not know that I have to concern myself with my Father's affairs? Then he went down with them and went to Nazareth, and he was subject to them. His mother kept all these things in her heart (Lk 2:46–52).

St. Joseph, when the child Jesus was lost for three days, you must have been plagued by worry while you sought him. Then, how happy you must have been when you and Mary found him in the Temple, sitting in the midst of the teachers, listening to them and asking them questions.

By this sorrow and joy of yours, ask the Lord to bless each member of my family and keep them safe from harm. Intercede before God for the family of nations so that discord may give way to harmony, hostility to forgiveness, rivalry to acceptance.

(Our Father, Hail Mary, Glory be...)

Novena to St. Joseph

Any one of the following prayers may be used according to the intention for the novena.

Prayer to Obtain a Special Favor

O glorious St. Joseph, steadfast follower of Jesus Christ, I am confident that your prayers for me will be graciously heard at the throne of God. To you I lift my heart and hands asking your powerful intercession to obtain from the compassionate heart of Jesus all the graces necessary for my spiritual and temporal well-being, particularly the grace of a happy death, and the special grace for which I now pray (*mention your request*).

St. Joseph, guardian of the Word Incarnate, by the love you bear for Jesus Christ, and for the glory of his name, hear my prayer and obtain my petitions. Amen.

----------••----------

Prayer in Time of Need

St. Joseph, patron of all who serve God in simplicity of heart and steadfast devotion, ask the Lord to fill my heart with the fire of his love. Awaken within me the virtues of integrity, simplicity, reverence, and gentleness, so that I may radiate God's love to those around me. Intercede for me in my time of particular need and obtain for me the favor I ask (*mention your request*). Blessed Joseph, be my protector in life and my consoler at the moment of death. Amen.

----------••----------

Prayer in Time of Difficulty

Holy Joseph, with steadfast confidence I come before you to seek your compassion and support. With fatherly care you accompanied and protected Jesus during his childhood. With the love and devotion of a spouse you cherished Mary his Mother. Now, through your intercession, assist me in this time of adversity. By the love you had for

Jesus and Mary on earth, I ask you to console me in my distress and present my petition to our heavenly Father *(mention your request)*.

Lord, give me the spirit of Joseph so that even amid my own hardships I can look beyond myself and reach out to others who are alone and suffering and thus be an instrument of your love and compassion. Amen.

---❦---

Prayer in Dark Times

To you, blessed Joseph, we come in our trials, and having asked the help of your most holy spouse, we confidently ask your patronage also. Through that love which bound you to the Immaculate Virgin Mother of God, and through the fatherly care with which you embraced the child Jesus, we humbly beg you to look kindly upon the inheritance which Jesus Christ has purchased by his blood, and to aid us in our necessities with your power and strength *(mention your request)*.

Most watchful guardian of the Holy Family, defend the followers of Jesus Christ; most loving father, defend us against the attacks of the evil one and assist us in our struggle against the power of darkness. As once you rescued the child Jesus from danger, so now protect God's holy Church from the power of Satan and from all harm. Shield, too, each one of us by your constant protection, so that, supported by your example and your help, we may be able to live as dedicated followers of Jesus Christ, die a holy death, and obtain eternal happiness in heaven. Amen.

(Adapted from common sources)

Various Prayers

St. Joseph, Patron of the Church

St. Joseph, be our protector. May your interior spirit of peace, silence, good work, and prayer for the cause of Holy Church always be our inspiration. May your spirit bring us joy in union with your blessed spouse, our sweet and gentle Immaculate Mother, and in the strong yet tender love of Jesus, the glorious and immortal King of all ages and peoples. Amen.

(Blessed Pope John XXIII)

Prayer for a Happy Death

St. Joseph, protector of the dying, I ask you to intercede for all the dying, and I invoke your assistance in the hour of my own death. You merited a happy passing by a holy life, and in your last hours you had the great consolation of being assisted by Jesus and Mary. Deliver me from sudden death; obtain for me the grace to imitate you in life, to detach my heart from everything worldly, and daily to gather treasures for the moment of my death. Obtain for me the grace to receive the sacrament of the sick well, and with Mary, fill my heart with sentiments of faith, hope, love, and sorrow for sins, so that I may breathe forth my soul in peace. Amen.

(Blessed James Alberione)

Prayer for the Dying

St. Joseph, foster father of Jesus Christ, and true spouse of the Virgin Mary, pray for us and for those who will die this day (or night).

Memorare to St. Joseph

Remember, O most chaste spouse of the Virgin Mary, that never has it been known that anyone who asked for your help or sought your intercession was left unaided. Inspired by this confidence, I commend myself to you and beg your protection. Despise not my petition, dear foster father of our Redeemer, but hear and answer my prayer. Amen.

(From common sources)

------ ✥ ------

A Worker's Prayer

St. Joseph, example for all those who work to support themselves and their families, obtain for me the grace to labor with thankfulness and joy. Grant that I may consider my daily endeavors as opportunities to use and develop the gifts of nature and grace I have received from God. In the workplace may I mirror your virtues of integrity, moderation, patience, and inner peace, treating my co-workers with kindness and respect. May all I do and say lead others to the Lord and bring honor to God's name. Amen.

------ ✥ ------

Prayer for One's Family

Heavenly Father, I thank you for the gift of my family and for the many joys and blessings that have come to me through each of them. Help me to appreciate the uniqueness of each while celebrating the diversity of all. Through the intercession of St. Joseph, foster father of your Son, I ask you to protect my family from the evils of this world. Grant us all the power to forgive when we have been hurt and the humility to ask for forgiveness when we have caused pain. Unite us in the love of your Son, Jesus, so that we may be a sign of the unity you desire for all humanity.

St. Joseph, intercede for us. Amen.

Prayer of Praise and Thanksgiving

It is fitting for us to praise and thank God for the graces and privileges he has bestowed upon the saints. Devotees of St. Joseph may pray the following act of thanksgiving during the novena.

Lord Jesus, I praise, glorify, and bless you for all the graces and privileges you have bestowed upon Joseph, your foster father and servant. By his merits grant me your grace, and through his intercession help me in all my needs. At the hour of my death be with me until that time when I can join the saints in heaven to praise you forever and ever. Amen.

Litany of St. Joseph

Lord, have mercy on us.
Christ, have mercy on us.
Lord, have mercy on us.
Christ, hear us.
Christ, graciously hear us.

God, the Father of heaven, *have mercy on us.*
God the Son, Redeemer of the world,
    have mercy on us.
God the Holy Spirit, *have mercy on us.*
Holy Trinity, one God, *have mercy on us.*

Holy Mary, *pray for us.*
St. Joseph, *pray for us.*
Esteemed offspring of David, *pray for us.*
Light of patriarchs, *pray for us.*
Faithful spouse of the Mother of God, *pray for us.*
Foster father of the Son of God, *pray for us.*
Guardian of the Holy Family, *pray for us.*
Joseph most just, *pray for us.*
Joseph most chaste, *pray for us.*
Joseph most prudent, *pray for us.*
Joseph most strong, *pray for us.*
Joseph most obedient, *pray for us.*

Joseph most faithful, *pray for us.*
Mirror of patience, *pray for us.*
Lover of poverty, *pray for us.*
Model of workers, *pray for us.*
Glory of home life, *pray for us.*
Guardian of virgins, *pray for us.*
Mainstay of families, *pray for us.*
Hope of the sick and suffering, *pray for us.*
Consoler of the dying, *pray for us.*
Protector of the Universal Church, *pray for us.*

Lamb of God, you take away the sins of the world,
    spare us, O Lord.
Lamb of God, you take away the sins of the world,
    graciously hear us, O Lord.
Lamb of God, you take away the sins of the world,
    have mercy on us.

V. The Lord made him guardian of his household,
R. His faithful and prudent servant.

Let us pray.
O God, in your providence you chose blessed Joseph to be the spouse of your most holy Mother. Grant that we may be worthy of the intercession of him whom we honor as our protector. We ask this through Christ, your Son. Amen.

(Adapted from common sources)

Evening Prayer

As this day draws to a close, we place ourselves in an attitude of thanksgiving. We take time to express our gratitude to a loving God for his abiding presence. We thank him for the gift of the day and all it has brought with it. We thank him for all the things we were able to achieve throughout the day, and we entrust to him the concerns we have for tomorrow.

From the rising to the setting of the sun,
may the name of the Lord be praised.
Glory be to the Father, and to the Son, and to the
    Holy Spirit,
as it was in the beginning, is now, and will be
    forever. Amen.

Take a few moments for a brief examination of conscience. Reflect on the ways God acted in your life today, how you responded to his invitations to think, speak, and act in a more Christ-like manner, and in what ways you would like to be a more faithful disciple tomorrow.

Lord, in your great love have mercy.
For the times I acted or spoke unkindly toward others.
Lord, have mercy.
For the times I was ungenerous with my time and talents.
Christ, have mercy.
For the times I was unwelcoming or unforgiving.
Lord, have mercy.
For the times... *(any other petitions for pardon).*

(Or any other Act of Sorrow.)

Psalm 67

May God bless us and may all the ends of the earth worship him.

May God be gracious to us and bless us.
May he let his face shine upon us,
that your way may be known on earth;
and your salvation, among all nations.
Let the peoples praise you, O God,
let all the peoples praise you.
Let the nations sing and shout with joy

for you judge the peoples with righteousness,
and guide the nations on the earth.
Let the peoples praise you, O God,
let all the peoples praise you.
The earth has brought forth its fruit.
May God, our God, bless us.
May God indeed bless us,
and may all the ends of the earth revere him.

The Word of God
John 15:4–5

God, who dwells within each of us, desires to be shared with others. But this is only possible if we make ourselves available to do God's work. How awesome to know that the Lord can act through us if we are willing!

"Abide in me, and I will abide in you.
Just as the branch cannot bear fruit on its own
unless it remains on the vine,
Likewise *you* cannot unless you abide in me.
I am the vine, you are the branches.
Whoever abides in me, and I in him,
He it is who bears much fruit,
For apart from me you can do nothing."

Lord, teach me your paths; lead me in your truth.

In prayer we bring before the Lord our own needs and the needs of those we love. We take time to consider the needs of the world and intercede for those who do not or cannot pray. We offer petitions for the improvement of the human condition so that our world will be a better place to live, and all people may contribute to building up God's kingdom here on earth.

Intercessions

$\mathcal{G}$ood and gracious God, we thank you for the gifts you have given us this day. With confidence in your loving care, we present to you our needs and the needs of all your people

Response: Lord, hear our prayer through the intercession of St. Joseph.

For Church leaders and those who minister in your name: may they lead lives of holiness and seek to be true witnesses to the gospel message of love and compassion. **R.**

For world leaders: may they govern with integrity and justice so that all peoples may live in peace and dignity. **R.**

For the poor, the homeless, refugees, and all who live on the margins of society: may they know the comfort of God and the help and support of the human family. **R.**

For those involved in peace efforts throughout the world: may their labors be effective and blessed with God's love. **R.**

For all mothers and fathers: may the Spirit grant them the love, wisdom, and courage they need to form their children as disciples of Jesus. **R.**

For the elderly, the homebound, and the terminally ill: may they find comfort in God's love for them and support from compassionate friends and caregivers. **R.**

For those who suffer in body, mind, or spirit: may they experience the compassionate touch of the Divine Healer. **R.**

For the faithful departed: may they enjoy the peace and happiness of heaven. **R.**

(Add any other spontaneous intentions and your particular intentions for this novena.)

Conclude your intercessions by praying to our heavenly Father in the words Jesus taught us:

Our Father, who art in heaven...

Closing Prayer

Gracious and loving God, as evening falls and this day draws to a close, remain with us. Bring us safely through the night so that with the coming of dawn we may give you praise and serve you more faithfully. We ask this through Christ, your Son. Amen.

Mary, Jesus' Mother and ours, is always ready to intercede for those who ask her help.

Hail, Holy Queen, Mother of mercy, our life, our sweetness, and our hope! To you we cry, poor banished children of Eve. To you we send up our sighs, mourning, and weeping in this valley of tears. Turn then, most gracious advocate, your eyes of mercy toward us, and after this our exile, show to us the blessed fruit of your womb, Jesus. O clement, O loving, O sweet Virgin Mary.

May God's blessing remain with us forever. In the name of the Father, and of the Son, and of the Holy Spirit. Amen.

BOOKS & MEDIA

The Daughters of St. Paul operate book and media centers at the following addresses. Visit, call, or write the one nearest you today, or find us at www.paulinestore.org.

CALIFORNIA
3908 Sepulveda Blvd, Culver City, CA 90230   310-397-8676
935 Brewster Avenue, Redwood City, CA 94063   650-369-4230

FLORIDA
145 S.W. 107th Avenue, Miami, FL 33174   305-559-6715

HAWAII
1143 Bishop Street, Honolulu, HI 96813   808-521-2731

ILLINOIS
172 North Michigan Avenue, Chicago, IL 60601   312-346-4228

LOUISIANA
4403 Veterans Memorial Blvd, Metairie, LA 70006   504-887-7631

MASSACHUSETTS
885 Providence Hwy, Dedham, MA 02026   781-326-5385

MISSOURI
9804 Watson Road, St. Louis, MO 63126   314-965-3512

NEW YORK
64 W. 38th Street, New York, NY 10018   212-754-1110

SOUTH CAROLINA
243 King Street, Charleston, SC 29401   843-577-0175

TEXAS
Currently no book center; for parish exhibits or outreach evangelization, contact: 210-569-0500, or SanAntonio@paulinemedia.com, or P.O. Box 761416, San Antonio, TX 78245

VIRGINIA
1025 King Street, Alexandria, VA 22314   703-549-3806

CANADA
3022 Dufferin Street, Toronto, ON M6B 3T5   416-781-9131